MW00928363

Mindfulness Exercises

Alfred James

Fourth Edition.

CONTENTS

About the Author

Alfred James was born in London in 1978. A student of Eastern philosophy, James teaches mindfulness as a way of coping with stress and anxiety, and as a pathway to self-acceptance.

Using a combination of positive habits, conscious thinking and meditation practices, he helps people release attachment to the past and worry over the future, and instead find opportunity and contentment in the present moment.

James' work continues to be used by therapists and medical practitioners to help those attending PTSD support groups, anger management programs, and addiction recovery, as well as being used by thousands of individuals to manage anxiety and stress.

He has been featured on a number of notable media platforms, including *The Huffington Post, The Guardian, Mindful Magazine,* and *BBC Radio.*

Author's Note

The term 'mindfulness exercises' is usually met with some resistance, which stands to reason. The majority of us lead such busy lives that we have precious little time for anything else, let alone more exercise!

But our busyness is the exact reason we should make time for this practice. Mindfulness exercises offer us respite from our relentless *doing*. These exercises provide a sanctuary away from the stress and constant striving; a place where we can stop, take a deep breath and truly notice what's going on, both externally and internally within the self.

We are so busy *doing* that our minds are seldom present to appreciate our reality, and rarely conscious enough to seize the opportunity presented in the now. We are constantly striving to be somewhere else: somewhere better, somewhere more prosperous, somewhere more glamorous. But what's the point of wanting to be elsewhere if, when you get there, you continue to feel the same way?

We find ourselves constantly living in the future: when I graduate… when I get a new job…when the kids leave home… when I have paid off the house… when I retire…

This narrative of modern life is responsible for much of our suffering: the stress we endure, the anxiety we suffer, the sleepless nights we battle, the restlessness that torments us and the emptiness we find in our quest for more than we need.

This continual striving for the next goal – the next achievement, the next landmark on our journey – deceives us and robs us of our potential to find our purpose and place in life, and ultimately of our chance to find inner peace.

Amidst our daily striving, we neglect the reality that death becomes us all. We have no idea when or how, but death is inevitable, a destiny we were born to fulfil. If we're lucky, death will follow sometime after retirement, and not long after we realise that for all we have achieved we understand very little about ourselves. Only then do we realise that amidst all the *doing*, we have neglected the opportunity to really understand and appreciate life.

The biggest tragedy of life is not death, but that so many people die having never really lived, quite simply because they weren't present enough to truly appreciate and understand the experience.

"But I'm squeezing in as much as I can before my time comes", I hear you say. But ask yourself: what is the point in owning a hundred diamonds if you have never taken the time to truly appreciate the sparkle of one?

The true gems of life are easily missed when the mind isn't present enough to realise their beauty.

Mindfulness exercises prompt us to stop in our tracks and engage in truly noticing life, something sorely neglected in our autopilot lives. Mindfulness exercises help us purposely observe our inner and outer world experience, helping us understand how and why we think and feel the way we do.

When we step into the present and bring the mind home in this way, we cultivate a deeper understanding of our connection with the world. A transparent awareness engulfs our being, enabling us to resolve inner and external conflicts with non-judgmental reasoning, and helping us develop compassion and loving-kindness for all sentient beings.

This self-liberating experience forms an essential foundation for seeing the interdependent one consciousness that binds us all in Mother Nature's clasp. We are in turn rewarded with a greater understanding of our purpose and place in the world.

Mindfulness exercises form a holistic means of coping with mental suffering, assisting with the management of sadness, depression, loss, anger, fear, anxiety and the general stress and uncertainty caused by the pressures of modern living.

By re-centring the mind through different forms of meditation, we develop a mental clarity that brings with it a more reliable compass to lead us through life's unpredictable landscape.

When we take time in this way to create a neutral connection with the world, away from the endless sporadic evaluation and judgement that pulls the mind in different directions throughout the day, an important truth unveils itself: in rushing around, frantically trying to achieve greater success and laying plans for a better future, worrying over what might happen if and when, and regretting past actions – we have been missing out on life.

We suddenly realise that we have been so busy living in moments that don't exist that we have neglected the life we should be living in the now. Moreover, we realise that we have lost sight of who we are, of the person playing the role in this mind and body, of the things that make us happy, of the non-material aspects of life that bring us true contentment, of the spiritual prosperity capable of tempering our empty desires and giving us the inner peace we unknowingly seek.

As we peel back the delusion of our unfounded preconceptions and unconscious conditioning, we realise that there is nothing to strive for because *this is it*. This is life, in this moment, happening right now. This is all that exists, and all that has ever existed. This moment is the result of all previous thought and action. It is absolutely perfect as it is, and absolutely as it was meant to be.

Seen fully clothed, life is a perpetual book of confusion; its chapters filled with blessed beginnings and tragic endings. Seen in its nakedness, life is a timeless, perfect moment, effortlessly bound together by one interdependent consciousness.

By seeing life in this way, we are able to find a sanctuary of inner peace that enables us to move forward calmly, positively and with clear seeing. Subsequently, we open up a wealth of possibility and opportunity with every step we take.

It is easy to confuse taking time out to be present with inaction. In fact, a popular misconception is that living through moment-to-moment awareness prevents you from setting goals and being productive. This isn't true. In fact, you'll be surprised at how much more productive you'll become when you start practising mindfulness exercises on a daily basis.

When we stand still and purposefully notice what is going on in the mind without judgement; when we interrupt the internal narration and external projection and open our eyes to the true nature of things; when we start living in this moment instead of constantly thinking about one that is yet to exist; we become undistracted and untangled from the self-limiting thoughts preventing us from taking positive action.

Cultivating a true awareness of self dissolves the mental barriers that prevent self-actualisation. You will begin to see that the large majority of your thoughts are a hindrance and cause emotional fragility and physical inaction. You will begin to see that the mind has a powerful ability to jade your perception of what you should be feeling or doing. When you stop looking forwards and backwards and stand still to observe your thoughts, feelings and senses, a mental clarity will arise that equips you with the inspiration, intuition and positivity to move forward prosperously, one step at a time. When you let go of wanting to get this moment over with as quickly as possible to reach a potentially better one, and let go of the continual dissatisfaction at not owning the things you desire, you will discover an effortless contentment in this moment and the next.

If we only ever desire better than we have, we will never be truly content. Yet we are taught to live this way, to continually strive for the next best thing – even though the resources we have may perfectly serve our needs as they are. This way of living promotes stress and anxiety, emptiness, dissatisfaction and a perpetual confusion that prevents us from fully enjoying our lives. If we live in the shadow of the unobtainable, if we allow ourselves to be driven by desire, then of course life becomes a disappointment. Our cup will become emptier with every fill. We will never feel satisfied or comfortable.

This doesn't mean we shouldn't aspire to better our circumstances or ourselves – quite the contrary. Cultivating mindfulness brings into our awareness the truth that if we don't start accepting, experiencing, appreciating and living life in the now, we will remain on the side-line and be left out of the game, so to speak. And a football player cannot influence a game from the bench.

The purpose of practising mindfulness is to fall awake into the world, not to stop progress or prevent aspiration. It is about saying; "I'm not going to let negative thoughts of the past and self-limiting predictions of the future prevent me from being happy. And all those things I keep wishing would happen, I am going to be conscious enough to create and fully enjoy them, moment-by-moment, step-by-step, lesson-by-lesson".

Mindfulness exercises free the mind and realign us with Mother Nature, rescuing us from the delusional belief that once we reach that next goal, own that new thing or find that right person we will suddenly realise lasting happiness and inner peace, which we know all too well from experience just isn't true.

The exercises set out in this guide will be of particular help to those suffering from stress, anxiety, depression, sleeplessness, lack of motivation and other related suffering of the mind. The exercises can be completed individually or conducted in groups, and can be used in place of, or in addition to, traditional meditation practice.

Whenever you feel overwhelmed with your mind's misleading projections, whenever you sense the need to take a rest from the striving and grasping causing you to feel stressed, frustrated and uncomfortable, choose the mindfulness exercise best suited to your circumstances and bring your mind home to rest in the peaceful awareness of the present moment.

Alfred James.

1. Self-Awareness

Watching the Breath of Life

The breath is the fine line between life and death. It is a powerful, essential function of life that sweeps through all sentient beings. The breath is the one thing that makes every sentient being equal, no matter its perceived intelligence or capability. But because breathing comes so easily to us when we are in good health, we naturally take its function for granted and seldom engage in using it to our full advantage.

The breath isn't just our life force, though. It has an incredible ability to change the way we think and feel; thus the saying 'take a deep breath'. When in a state of anxiety, focussing on slowing the breath's tempo has a profound affect on the body's disposition. As you breathe in deeply, the diaphragm drops downward, making room for your lungs to expand as they fill with air. As you breathe out, the diaphragm presses back upward against your lungs, helping to expel not just carbon dioxide but also anxiety and tension from the body. Breathing deeply in this way also slows heart rate and helps stabilise blood pressure.

In meditation, we use the breath as a tool to release negative energy, cultivate relaxation and prepare the mind for stillness. We use the breath to reconnect us with a pure awareness of what is, to bring us into the present moment and realign us with Mother Nature.

Focusing on the breath helps us enter a meditative state, assisting us in finding the mental spaciousness required to release attachment and aversion. In essence, the breath is used to bring the mind home and free us from the grasping that causes our day-to-day mental suffering.

In this first exercise, we're going to use the breath to cultivate a profound awareness of existence. This is a mentally liberating exercise that will help you find a sanctuary of peace in the present moment. This exercise is best suited to a place of quiet, where you feel comfortable enough to close your eyes and relax for ten minutes. I recommend sitting in the garden, or the park if the weather is suitable. If you can't go outside, use a quiet room in your home.

Step 1:

Sit down on the floor or on a chair. If you are unable to sit, stay standing – just make sure you feel comfortable. Don't lie down, as you don't want to tempt the brain into falling asleep. If you can, assume a cross-legged meditation (lotus) position. This position is highly conducive to optimal breathing and will help you get the most from this exercise.

Step 2:

Once you are comfortable, close your eyes. Begin by taking slow, deep breaths. Breathe in through your nose, and then effortlessly out through your mouth.

After a couple of minutes, gradually allow your breathing cycle to lengthen. Breathe in for approximately three seconds and then exhale for the same. Don't strain to hold your breath at any point; just settle into a deep rhythm that you feel comfortable with.

Step 3:

Focus solely on your breathing, ignoring your thought stream and internal narrator. Let thoughts come and go of their own will, noticing them for what they are (just thoughts) and allowing them to drift away as you continue to focus on your breath. If you are distracted by an external noise, do the same; simply notice it for what it is and let it drift away into the atmosphere. If you recognise a sound that begins to pull at your attention, identify it, let it go and return to the breath. The purpose of this exercise is to connect fully with your breath, taking leave from all external distraction.

Step 4:

Visualise the breath swirling through the inside of your body and flowing back out through your mouth. Watch it through the inhalation and exhalation cycle, feeling its texture and power flow through your being. Witness the border of life and death in the small window when your breath completely leaves your body, and then revel in the beauty of existence as you are once again filled with its presence.

Do this exercise for as long as you feel engaged with the breath. If you lose the connection but wish to continue, simply go back to Step 1 and start over. You will probably manage between 2-4 minutes in your first few sittings. However, in time you will find yourself effortlessly watching the breath for up to twenty minutes.

Notes

This exercise will leave you feeling present, spacious and revitalised in mind and body. To merge with one's breath in such a way is a joyous feeling, one that opens a gateway to higher spiritual consciousness and reconnects you with the true essence of life. Regular practice will cultivate a deeper appreciation of the gift of life, and of the interconnectedness of the life-death cycle.

2. Freeing the Mind

Expelling Negativity

When it feels like the world is conspiring against us, we become susceptible to negative thought patterns and self-limiting behaviours. We forget the good that came before the bad period and, in our emotional state, forget that while we have limited control over external circumstances, we can control the way we respond. We have the power to make a difference by seizing the moment, and each action we take directly affects the next.

The following exercise will help remove your preoccupation with negative past experiences by encouraging your mind to realise the abundance of opportunity presented in the now. Once the mental fog begins to clear, you will see the bigger, more positive picture and start attracting positive energy back into your life.

Step 1:

Find a comfortable seat and sit down, either indoors or outdoors. Don't do anything except sit down: don't turn on the television, don't look at the clock and don't look at your mobile phone. Do nothing. Just be as you are in mind and body.

Step 2:

Close your eyes and turn your attention to the stream of thoughts running through your mind. Visualise the stream of thoughts as flowing water carrying the constant projections of your mind in its constancy. Now, can you see that bank on the side of the stream? Take a seat there and watch the stream for a while.

Objectively observe your thoughts as they are carried past. Once you are fully observing the stream, begin identifying your negative thoughts. Because these negative thoughts have recently been dominating your awareness, they may appear to stop and tread water in the stream, craving your attention and seeking to dominate your awareness. Single them out from the positive thoughts by labelling them "negative". When you identify one, or one makes itself known by trying to dominate your awareness, don't struggle with it. Don't allow the thought to penetrate your objective viewpoint or to annoy or anger you. Simply stay seated on the bank and label the thought for what it is.

Once you've labelled it, fish the thought out of the stream and place it on the bank to your left-hand side. Do this with each negative thought you identify.

Each time you place a negative thought on the bank, return to the thought stream and again observe the flow objectively, allowing positive thoughts to pass by untroubled.

Step 3:

Take a minute to notice that all the thoughts in the stream, whether positive or negative, have something in common: when seen from a neutral perspective, they are all mere perceptions, judgements and evaluations. They are projections of the mind based on situations, people and other related thoughts. In this respect, the positive thoughts are no different to the negative thoughts. A thought is therefore only as powerful as the attention you give it.

Contemplate this for a minute or two while you continue to sit on the bank. If one of the negative thoughts beside you should fall back into the stream, simply fish it out and put it back on the bank to the left-hand side.

Step 4:

As the stream flows past, you will see lots of positive thoughts that reflect the present: images of your family and friends, a pet perhaps, circumstances relating to your career, your love for your partner and other positive aspects of your life. Choose the positive thoughts you most value and begin fishing them out, placing them to your right-hand side on the bank. Fish approximately the same number of positive thoughts out of the stream as you have negative thoughts. Don't worry if you can't remember how many of each you have; it's not important.

Step 5:

Now look to your left at the negative thoughts beside you, and then to your right side at the positive thoughts. Ponder the two groups of thoughts for a minute. Consider what you believe to be worth holding onto in this moment. Think about the reality of now. Think about what really matters for you going forward in life. Consider the things you cherish in your life, the things that bring you sustainable happiness. See the negative thoughts for what they are: bad memories and future worries that have no reality in the present. These thoughts can only exist if you hold onto them. They have either expired or are yet to exist; only your mind gives them a reality.

The positive thoughts, on the other hand, have significant relevance. They are based on love, compassion and feelings of happiness, of things that empower you to be a better person and enjoy your life.

The thoughts you choose to hold onto will determine the narrative in your mind and ultimately your actions in everyday life. Negative thoughts breed negative energy and detract from your ability to think clearly and see positively. By letting go of negative thoughts, positive thoughts can be appreciated and utilised at a greater level of awareness.

Step 6:

Now, one by one, throw the negative thoughts back into the stream. Watch them sink back into the endless freeway of thoughts flowing through your mind. Watch them dissolve into nothingness, swallowed by the past and forgotten by your present. Now, one by one, pick up each positive thought and put them in your pocket (into your awareness).

Open your eyes and allow yourself to beam a big smile. Make it your duty today to appreciate and act on each positive thought that you have fished out of the stream. For example, if you thought of your partner, reach out to him or her with a loving gesture. If you thought of your dog, then go for a long walk in the park together. If you thought of your children or your best friend, then make arrangements to spend some quality time together as soon as possible.

Notes

Practising this exercise on a regular basis will give you the ability to partition your thoughts during challenging times. You will be able to access your thought stream on demand and quickly eliminate negative, unhelpful thoughts that limit clear thinking and good decision-making.

Being able to cultivate and tap into mental clarity in this way teaches you the art of expelling negative energy from your mind. This will enable you to adeptly deal with stressful and traumatic situations by improving your ability to cope in an emotionally balanced, rational and compassionate way.

3. Being Present

Pacing the Square of Reality

This next exercise brings with it a profound reminder that *this* is all there is. No matter where your desire is trying to lead you, there is no better place to be, and no better or worse moment worth thinking about than the present moment. Nothing exists except the now.

By using a controlled walking meditation, we are able to find peace in a confined space. With limited external distraction and only the simple task of putting one foot in front of the other, we are presented with the opportunity to turn the search inwards. In the repetitive motion of our steps, we come face to face with the vacuous and unproductive nature of the grasping mind. The grasping mind is never content in the now and finds nothing wholly satisfying. But with each step of this exercise, we have the opportunity to release the mind's rueing of the past and anxieties of the future and tame it into satisfaction with what *is*.

We all feel the occasional compulsion to pace up and down, usually when mulling over a decision, or as a way to calm our frustration or temper our disappointment. But this type of pacing is different. In this situation we pace hard and without consideration of a boundary. The mind is frantic and our actions are unmeasured. This serves to make us more anxious and stressed. In this exercise, however, you will learn how to use the concept of pacing to slow the world down and see its simple reality. You will empty your mind and become rooted in the present moment.

Each step in this exercise represents a moment in time, which in turn represents life: a series of interdependent moments that, when seen in their nakedness, transpire as one perpetual, never-ending moment. In this realisation, the illusion of time fades away and the essence of what it means to be present reveals itself in all its beauty.

Step 1:

This exercise can be practised in any place where you have an unobstructed area that allows you to walk for approximately five metres in each direction.

First, create a boundary on the floor. A tiled floor (or other type of floor that has notable markings) is preferable because you'll be able to visually create a boundary using the lines of the tiles. If the floor lacks visual markings, feel free to use markers. The square you pace should be roughly equal on each side.

Take off your shoes and socks, and make sure you are wearing comfortable (preferably loose) clothing. Put your phone on silent or, better still, put it away completely so that you aren't aware of its presence. Whether you're at home or at work, let those likely to interrupt you know that you want to remain undisturbed for the next ten minutes.

Step 2:

Once you have mapped out your square, begin slowly pacing its perimeter with slow, controlled steps. Look down at the floor and keep your eyes focussed just in front of your feet. Don't worry if you don't have markings on the floor to follow, simply feel your way through the exercise and create an imaginary perimeter to follow.

Step 3:

Keep pacing for as long as you feel engaged. There is absolutely no goal to your movement, and nothing you should be thinking or feeling other than what naturally enters your mental space. Let thoughts come and go as they please and allow tension, stress and anxiety to fall away from your being as you gently take each step. Let negative emotions dissolve in the knowledge that nothing matters except walking this square in this moment. All you have to do is focus on slowly pacing the perimeter of your square.

Notes

On the face of it, this exercise seems somewhat pointless. I mean, why walk slowly around a square for ten minutes or more – is that not a waste of time?

But once practised, you'll understand that the action itself quickly becomes insignificant. The repetition and purposeful attention to the task is merely the vehicle to a higher consciousness and deeper awareness of self that brings the mind into a state of stillness in the present.

Each step represents life itself, a series of moments, seamlessly strung together to create one never-ending present.

Learning to be attentive to this small square and carefully observing each single step along its boundary will lead you to a profound self-harmony, evoking peace of mind. You will realise that mental balance and clarity of mind is only ever a simple step away.

4. Releasing Attachment

Tech-Free for a Day

Whether at home watching television, glued to the computer at work or on the go frantically sending messages across social media from a phone, digital devices play a massive part in our lives.

We have become so attached to these devices that in many ways they are an extension of our identity. From the brands we use to the profile names we choose and the apps we interact with, many of us would feel lost without our digital personality.

Modern technology is of course incredibly useful because it enhances our ability to communicate on a global scale. This is great for business and wonderful for staying in touch with friends and relatives. But socially, it is fundamentally changing the way we interact with each other. We spend less time speaking face-to-face, less time outside engaging with nature, and increasingly more time living in the pseudo reality of smartphones and computers.

With our heads buried in the digital world and our concentration scattered by pictures, messages and notifications at any given moment, we are increasingly distracted from the true nature of our existence. We become disconnected from ourselves and disengaged from humanity, neglecting the much-needed human interaction that enables us to cultivate valuable relationships.

Technology continues to bring wonderful opportunities to the world, but it is important to remain in touch with the *self* through the cultivation of spiritual consciousness. Otherwise we find ourselves driven by attachment and the compulsive instincts it triggers. We become unable to engage in conversation without wondering if we have any new emails or notification alerts. We become more interested in the lives of reality TV stars than our own, and subsequently neglect the nurture of our personal relationships and the needs of those less fortunate than ourselves.

Living without checking Facebook or watching television for 24 hours might sound like removing enjoyment from your life, but challenging yourself to complete this next exercise will bring about a liberating experience. You will be forced to let go of your reliance on technology and step back into the world of real social interaction.

The beauty of this exercise is that it will give your mind a chance to detach and defragment, to live a while without the distractions that constantly crave your attention in the vacuum of the digital world.

Step 1:

The first step is to make a commitment to limit your exposure to technology as much as possible for 24 hours. This is best done on a day when you don't need to use a computer or aren't waiting on an urgent phone call.

Start by cutting out the technology you can truthfully live without. Ask yourself: do I really need to carry my phone around today? Could I live without watching television tonight? Could I travel on the bus without my mp3 player? Could I leave the games console alone for just one night? Could I go offline for a day and step back into the real world instead?

Purposefully minimise your interaction with technology while increasing your interaction with people and the natural world.

Step 2:

If you are a television or gaming addict then no doubt this task will be fairly challenging. Suddenly there is no phone to fiddle with, no computer to switch on and no TV to slump in front of. So what will you do instead?

Try something different, something you'd like to do but only ever get as far as thinking about before being interrupted by a bleep on your phone. Start reading that book you bought ages ago, do a yoga session or go for a long walk in the park. Write a poem, paint a picture or play your guitar. Visit a friend you haven't had a face-to-face conversation with for some time, or spend time playing with your siblings and talking with your family. Whatever you do, interact in the world without technology as much as you can.

Step 3:

When you find yourself with nothing to do - in those moments when you would usually be checking your phone or watching television - try simply observing life. Notice everything that is happening around you when you aren't normally paying attention. Notice flowers in the garden, listen intently to birds singing in the trees, watch the motion of dogs running in the park, feel the breeze caressing your face as you sit on your doorstep. Observe the season and its contrast with the last. Visually inspect the colours of your environment and analyse the aspects of your world that usually pass by unnoticed. Non-judgmentally and purposefully observe, listen, feel, smell and embrace the world.

Notes

This exercise will challenge you to take leave of the digital world and reconnect with the natural world that supports your existence. Sure, technology is fun, but there is nothing more beautiful and soul fulfilling than interacting in the natural world.

It is so easy to miss life's wonders by burying your head in a phone, aimlessly scrolling through social media posts and starring at the television. This overindulgence in technology promotes a mindless, idle and ultimately disconnected state of being. By going tech-free for a day, you are giving yourself the opportunity to lift your head out of the digital cloud and realign with your purpose and place in the natural world – to do exactly what you were designed for.

5. Self-Realisation

Life Through the Eyes of an Ant

The lives of animals are generally considered by most to be of lesser significance. Ants are a prime example of this speciesism. Small and a potential annoyance, ants are widely seen as pests that want to eat our food and invade our homes.

You have probably never felt compelled to sit and watch a group of ants scurry around your feet; at least not since you were a child, anyway. I'm willing to bet that if you do, you'll think twice before squashing the next one that finds its way into your kitchen.

All animals are amazing in their own right, but ants are a particularly beautiful example of nature's greatness. The way ants work together as a community to navigate obstacles and hunt down and carry food is truly incredible.

In our position of earthly dominance, it is easy to forget the killing of an ant or the elimination of an entire nest in the garage. But once you study, understand and appreciate these creatures, it comes into conscience that ants are every bit as important to this world as we are.

The reality is that if Mother Nature decided it be so, the world would go on without humans, as it would without ants or any other animal. Recognising the equal value of every living creature humbles our existence and puts life in perspective. It realigns our outlook on the world by prompting us to remember that every animal has its rightful place in the cycle of life.

Life Through the Eyes of an Ant is an exercise that reconnects us with nature. It is simply about taking time out to appreciate that animals, no matter how small, are as wonderful and valuable as we are. Like ants, we come from the earth and to the earth we shall return.

If you have children, I strongly suggest doing this exercise together; it costs nothing and is a great way to introduce young minds to the wonders of the natural world.

Step 1:

The first step is to find some ants. Ants can usually be found near trees or under rocks, but if you can, try to locate some on a fence or narrow ledge in the garden. Once you have found some ants, place some bread, crisp or biscuit crumbs within a few inches of the ants.

Step 2:

Ants have four to five times more odour receptors than most other insects, so you won't have to wait too long for them to start interacting with the food. Once the ants start approaching the food, watch as others join in and begin their teamwork. Observe how they investigate the food and then organise themselves to carry the crumbs back to the nest. Watch how they assist each other when the load gets too heavy or is dropped. Watch closely as they carry out their allocated duties within the community. If you manage to find some ants on a fence or other narrow ledge, observe their agility skills and the way in which they intelligently work around each other within a confined space.

Step 3:

If the ants are a particularly small species, use a magnifying glass to study their actions. Focus in on one ant at a time. Watch as each ant uses its limbs to navigate the terrain and pick up food. Consider the character of each ant. Try to identify the bossy ant, the strong ant, the aggressive ant and the lazy ant. Kids will particularly enjoy using their imagination to liken the ants to people in this way.

Notes

I often say that to realise one's true place in the world is to realise that humans are no more important than ants. Ants have a home to rest and nest. They eat, communicate, work and function as part of a community, and spend their lives trying to survive and make the best of their environment. When seen in this way, ants are just like humans: they are beings operating interdependently in a huge, interconnected universe. We are all part of this cycle of life, and all of us have an equally important role to play.

6. Self-Discovery

Entering a Mindful Silence

To take a good look at yourself, one might suggest looking in the mirror. But this would mean looking only at the physical side of your being. And this is problematic, because when we see the reflection, we begin to make judgements based on the image we see. To really take a good look at ourselves, we need to look within. To understand the *self*, we need to go beyond visual evaluation.

Neither does it help to look to others for an understanding of who we are. Because when we base our understanding of the *self* on the opinions and expectations of others, we find ourselves living through an external interpretation that is not only misrepresented but beyond our control.

And so it is necessary to bring the mind home, to stop the external projection and turn the search inwards. A practical way of doing this is to take a vow of mindful silence for a controlled period of time. It is a profound experience to be alone with the *self* in this way. It leads us to confront the narrator of our actions and challenge emotional conflict without the optional escapism of verbal interaction. Controlled silence leads us into a state of observation, resulting in the cultivation of a true awareness of what is.

Engaging in a period of mindful silence isn't an easy task, particularly if you are someone who rarely goes a few minutes without speaking. So try this exercise for half an hour to begin with, and then extend the duration if you find it rewarding. There are some specific conditions to follow, so pay close attention to the steps below.

Step 1:

The goal is to be silent for a minimum of thirty minutes. You can choose to start the exercise when you feel like having some quiet time, or when you can schedule a time around your working day. You should find a place where you feel relaxed and are not likely to be distracted by others trying to talk to you.

Step 2:

It is important that you minimise distraction by confining your silence to a specific area. This might be your garden, a room in your home, or even the square you paced when performing Exercise 3 (*Being Present - Pacing the Square of Reality*).

Step 3:

The only three things you should do during this exercise are walk, sit and notice, nothing more. Remember that this exercise is more than just about being quiet. This is about silencing the distractions, which means taking leave from your normal routine and releasing yourself from material attachments like your car and your phone. The idea is to be alone with your awareness, to turn the mind inwards and confront your thoughts.

Notes

Being silent for thirty minutes or more might sound like an easy task, but it takes on a whole new meaning when you restrict yourself from doing anything other than sitting, walking and observing. During your silence you will observe feelings, thoughts and emotions objectively, as a spectator of your mind. You will be without the escapism of your voice and the company of others. You will be faced with the nakedness of your hopes, fears and insecurities, and at times confronted with difficult thoughts and questions. But you don't need to take any action. All you have to do is be silent and observe. Accept and let go of everything that comes into your awareness.

With regular practice, you will find that silence is no longer a scary place where the unknown lurks but a place of peace, a sanctuary where you are able to reassess, realign and recalibrate your awareness away from the haze of everyday distraction that scatters the mind. Like a computer, you are defragmenting and reorganising your files. The stillness you find within the silence will soon become your personal wellness retreat, a place where you are able to come home to yourself.

7. Self-Liberation

Freedom in the Wind

Because of our planetary dominance and high-tech world, we have become increasingly detached from the ecosystems supporting our existence. This is even truer for those living in the concrete jungle of urban environments. This disconnection from the natural world leads us into a false sense of being, one that makes us feel that we are in some way separate from Mother Nature.

Our experience of the natural world is partitioned, seen through the walls of a zoo or the lens of a nature documentary. Only when we are affected by natural disaster does it really hit home that we are as vulnerable to nature's forces as any other species.

The reality is that we are not a separate entity. We are not a higher power capable of existing outside of the natural world. We are, and will always remain, part of the interdependent, interconnected cycle of nature. We know this to be true because even the smallest alteration in the natural environment is capable of permanently changing our existence. A change of weather in one country can affect another many thousands of miles away, and the extinction of a small species of insect can in some way affect the most powerful predator at the top of the food chain.

We humans play just a small part in an ocean of powerful, intricate processes. This is not something we should fear or feel belittled by, but instead embrace and enjoy being a part of.

This next exercise is designed to help you realign with the creator, Mother Nature. It is time to exit the modern technological world and reconnect with your inner primal self.

For this exercise you will of course need to be outdoors. You will also need to find a place where the wind blows quite strongly. A hillside or beach is perfect, or you can wait for a really windy day and do this in the park or your garden.

Step 1:

Stand facing into the wind. Spread your arms out wide, as if you were about to embrace a loved one running towards you from afar. Close your eyes and let the wind smother your face. Tilt your head back slightly so the wind blows through your hair and whistles across the contours of your face. Don't resist the wind; submit to its power and let its energy consume you.

Step 2:

Feel the energy filling your body as you become empowered by this incredible force of nature. Visualise the energy flowing through your body, right down to your feet and then swirling around up into your legs, stomach and chest.

Step 3:

Now open your mouth and let out a primal roar. As loud as you can, release the energy and roar with all your might. Do not think twice about who might be listening or what you look like; just let it all go and roar like a lion.

Notes

This exercise is an exhilarating way to feel your intrinsic bond with nature. It's a fun way to let go and submit to the universe. It's also a great stress reliever. This exercise provides us with a wonderful reminder that we are born of Mother Nature and to her we shall return. Her energy flows through us at all times. When you feel a little down in the dumps, or begin questioning the point of life, use this exercise to re-establish your connection with the universe.

8. Appreciation (Mindful Eating)

The Raisin of Life

The majority of us are fortunate enough to live in a society of abundance, where we coast through life without truly appreciating our privilege.

Eating is one such area of life we take for granted. All too often we gobble down our food without tasting it properly, without appreciating the work we put in to be able to buy the food, and without a second thought for where it came from or who cultivated its existence.

In this exercise, we are going to explore mindful eating, as opposed to simply going through the motions of having something to eat. Instead of eating on autopilot, we are going to appreciate the gift of food and its importance to our existence in the cycle of life. You'll need some raisins, or a similar type of snack.

Step 1:

Pour out a small handful of raisins. Hold the raisins in one hand and use the other to feed yourself. Start by picking up one raisin and lifting it slowly towards your mouth. Watch it all the way to your mouth until it caresses your lips. From hand to mouth, observe its shape, colour and design. This process should take at least 30 seconds.

Step 2:

Place the raisin on your tongue. Do not bite down or chew. Leave the raisin on your tongue and notice the sensations in your body as your brain prepares for you to eat.

Step 3:

Now, still without chewing, use your tongue to roll the raisin around your mouth. As it moves from one side of your mouth to the other, close your eyes and feel its texture. Observe its flavour as the sweetness flows down to your taste buds through your saliva.

Step 4:

Notice the connection between your mind and body in this process of eating. Only a conscious decision to swallow now stands between consumption and fulfilment. Remain in limbo in this space for a minute or so, while considering where this raisin might have come from. Consider the process of its growing, harvesting, drying and packaging. Use your imagination to follow the raisin's journey from vine to mouth.

Step 5:

Now slowly chew the raisin. Focus on its texture and taste now that you have broken its skin. Observe any bodily sensations you feel as you prepare to consume the fruit. As you begin swallowing, visualise the fruit making its journey into your digestive system. Follow its pathway down your throat and through the body before it reaches the acids of your stomach.

Step 6:

Repeat the process, but this time focussing on the difference between this new raisin and the last. In the same way no two humans are the same, no two raisins, or any other fruit for that matter, are the same either. Do your best to notice the difference in shape and texture as you repeat the process. Finally, see how long you can patiently repeat this exercise with the remaining raisins in your hand.

Notes

The purpose of this exercise is to become present enough while eating to really appreciate food and its connection to your existence. By cultivating a conscious awareness of the privilege of having easy access to food, we are encouraged to be less greedy and share our abundance with others. Mindful eating also promotes better eating habits, prompting us to purposefully notice the types of food we are eating and the quantities we consume during each meal.

9. Understanding the Nature of Mind

Observing Your Thoughts

In order to free ourselves from the control of its scattered and grasping nature, we need to become aware of how the mind works. So in this exercise, we sit as an observer, taking time out to watch and notice the mind in operation.

The purpose of this exercise is to notice the type and volume of thoughts that occur, from a spectator's view of impartiality. This might sound easy, but you will soon see that separating your awareness - becoming the spectator - can be a trying task. The idea is to not become involved with your thoughts and simply observe the nature of your mind, as if it belonged to someone else.

In preparation for this exercise, engage your beginner's mind by considering the following questions for a minute or two:

- Where do your thoughts come from?
- Are thoughts created in your mind, or do they just appear of their own accord?
- Do you have any control over your thoughts?
- Can you choose your thoughts or filter the subjects you think about?

Step 1:

To partake in this exercise, you will need to stop everything you are doing: stop working, talking, moving, eating and any other action. The purpose is to be alone with your mind.

Sit down, make yourself comfortable and close your eyes. Don't distract your practice with a time limitation; feel your way through the exercise and stop when you've had enough.

Step 2:

Think of your thoughts like icons on the reel of a slot machine. In everyday life you are merged with the reel, stuck surfing on its cycle as it spins around. In this exercise, you are going to jump off the reel and pull up a stool by the side of the machine, as an observer.

Step 3

As you sit there watching the reel of thoughts spin, notice each thought as a spectator. Detach yourself from identifying with these thoughts as your own. If it helps, imagine that these thoughts belong to someone else – but not to anyone you know.

There are no expectations or goals in this exercise. If the reel suddenly stops spinning, just rest in that space and see what happens. Similarly, if the reel's movement becomes inconsistent, just watch and wait to see what happens next.

As an additional task, you may choose to spend some moments writing about the patterns and characteristics of the thoughts you experience. This serves as an additional way to gain a greater understanding of how your mind works.

Notes

You will quickly realise that it's practically impossible to keep up with the huge volume of thoughts that spin through your mind. You will also realise that the majority of these thoughts are trivial, unhelpful and often irrelevant. Only a handful of thoughts will contribute to your life with relevance and positivity, and it is these thoughts that you should focus on manifesting in your everyday reality.

So what does this tell us about the mind?

It tells us that the mind has a dual nature. There is the often delusional, scattered nature of mind, and the true (somewhat reliable) nature of mind. Thoughts projected by the delusional mind are generally unfounded evaluations and judgements that cause us to become caught up in attachment, desire and generally negative behaviours. These thoughts jade our perception of reality and prevent us from seeing clearly and taking positive action. By recognising this dual nature, and by practising meditation and mindfulness exercises such as this one, we can develop the ability to tame the grasping mind and better utilise the reliable mind. This in turn helps guide us more prosperously through life's landscape.

It is important to note that the intention of this exercise is not to try and stop thoughts occurring. We cannot prevent thoughts and there is no filter we can apply to determine the subject matter. However, being able to recognise unhelpful, negative and self-limiting thoughts enables us to reduce their influence over our actions. This allows us to focus our energy on positive thoughts that are conducive to our well-being and prosperity.

10. Being Here

Letting Go

Having worked your way through these mindfulness exercises, you will have probably noticed a reoccurring theme – *letting go*.

In one way or another, each one of these exercises encourages us to stop, detach and observe life; to let go of the wanting, the expecting, the predicting and the desiring. The purpose is to be present and truly engage with life in the now.

When we make a conscious decision to live in the now, we see that everything is here, as it should be, in this moment. And though we may use the word *moment* to define the now, the truth is that the present is always here; there is only one constant moment. There is no better place to get to, only a better present to create. Despite what the delusional mind tries to tell us, true freedom and self-actualisation always reside in the now. Embracing this reality is all the knowledge you need to find contentedness.

And so, for this last exercise, there is only one step to complete, and that is to simply let go:

- Let go of wanting to be elsewhere.
- Let go of wanting to be someone else.
- Let go of wanting more than you have.
- Let go of your expectations.
- Let go of your expectations of others.
- Let go of your insecurities.
- Let go of your fears.
- Let go of your perceptions.
- Let go of your judgements.

- Let go of what you think you know.

Allow yourself to be fully here, in the present moment. Accept who you are. Accept your feelings, good or bad. Let go of wanting, hoping or believing. Instead, purposefully live through what you know to be true in this moment, not through your experiences of the past or expectations of the future.

Everything we need to be doing, everything we need to know, and every person we need to help and love is right here, in the now. Let go of grasping towards the future and worrying about what might happen, and instead take action now to create a better present.

Copyright Notice